See the U.S.A.

My First Backseat Books®

Copyright ©1997 by Rand McNally and Company. All rights reserved. Published and printed in the U.S.A.

Color in all the states you'll visit across the U.S.A.

WELCOME to The Northeast!

Circle the states that begin with M.
Put an X on the states that begin with N.

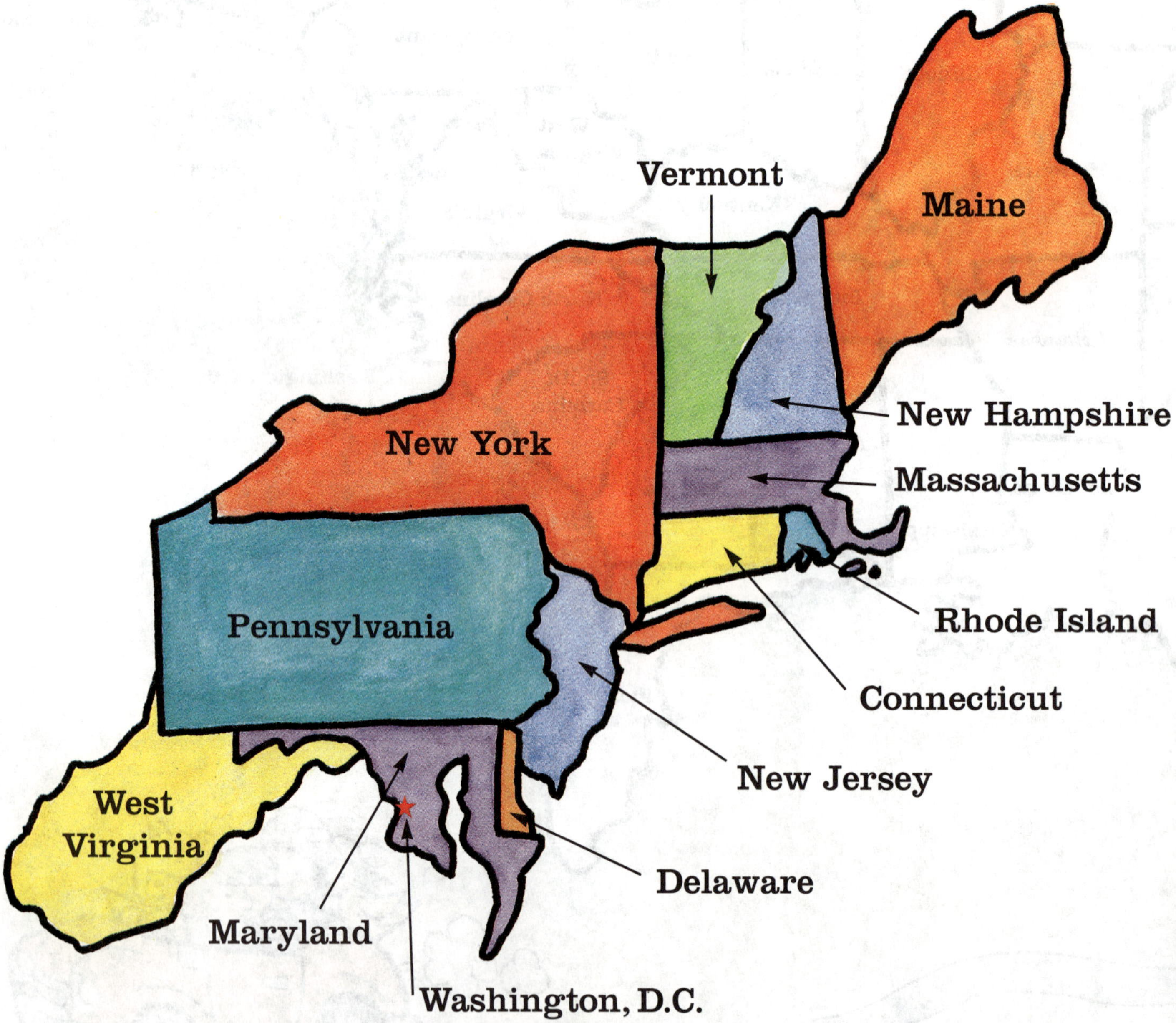

Circle all the things that are red on this **Vermont** ski slope.

It's fall in **New Hampshire!**

Help Paul Revere find his way home through the streets of Boston, **Massachusetts.**

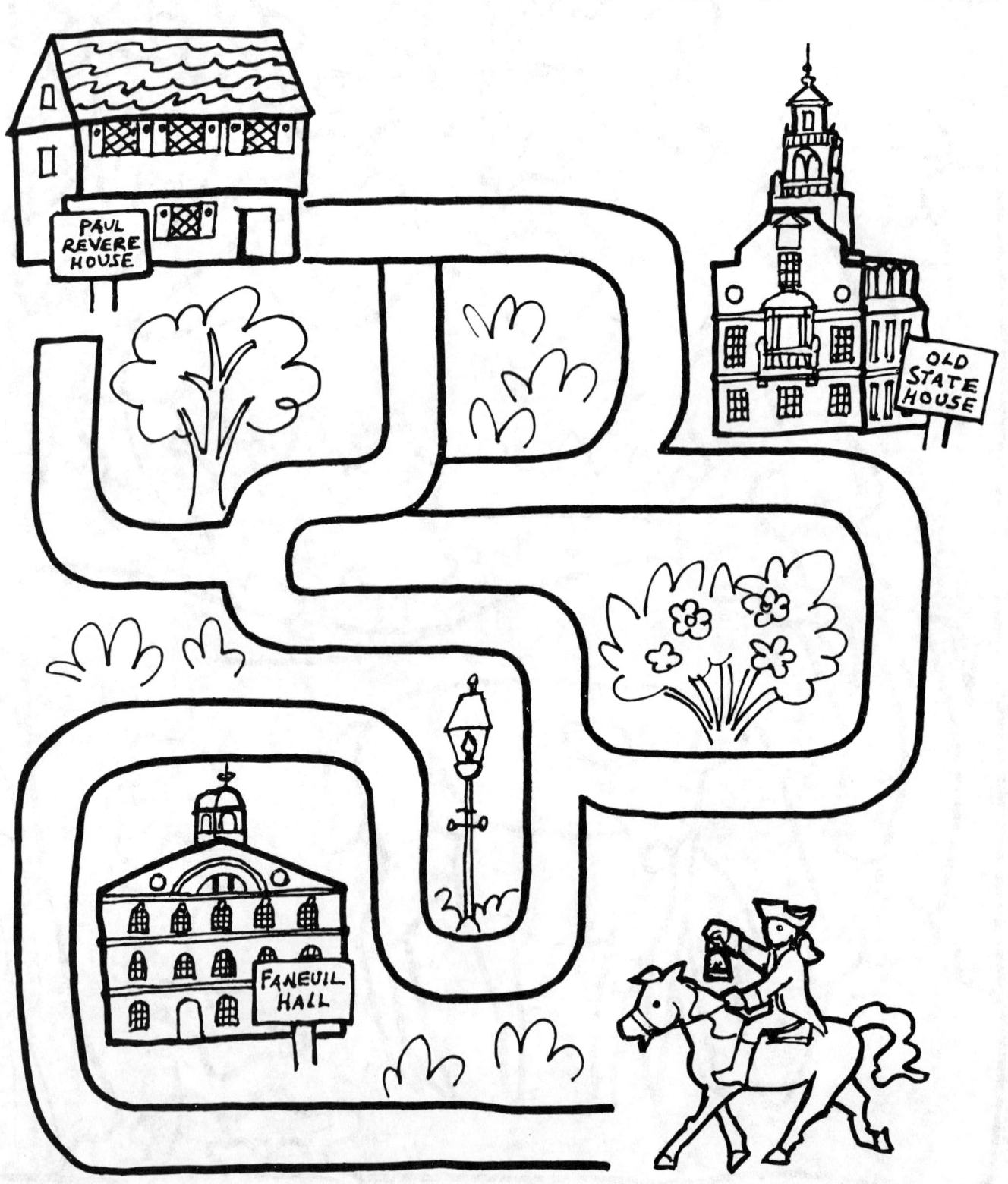

What's going on at this seaport in **Connecticut**? Circle seven things that are wrong.

Use the code to color in these **Rhode Island** sailors.

1=blue   2=green   3=red   4=yellow   5=brown

Color the picture of the Statue of Liberty in **New York**.

**What's the state bird of New Jersey?
The goldfinch!**

What's this little mouse swinging on in Philadelphia, **Pennsylvania**? Connect the dots from 1 to 22 to find out.

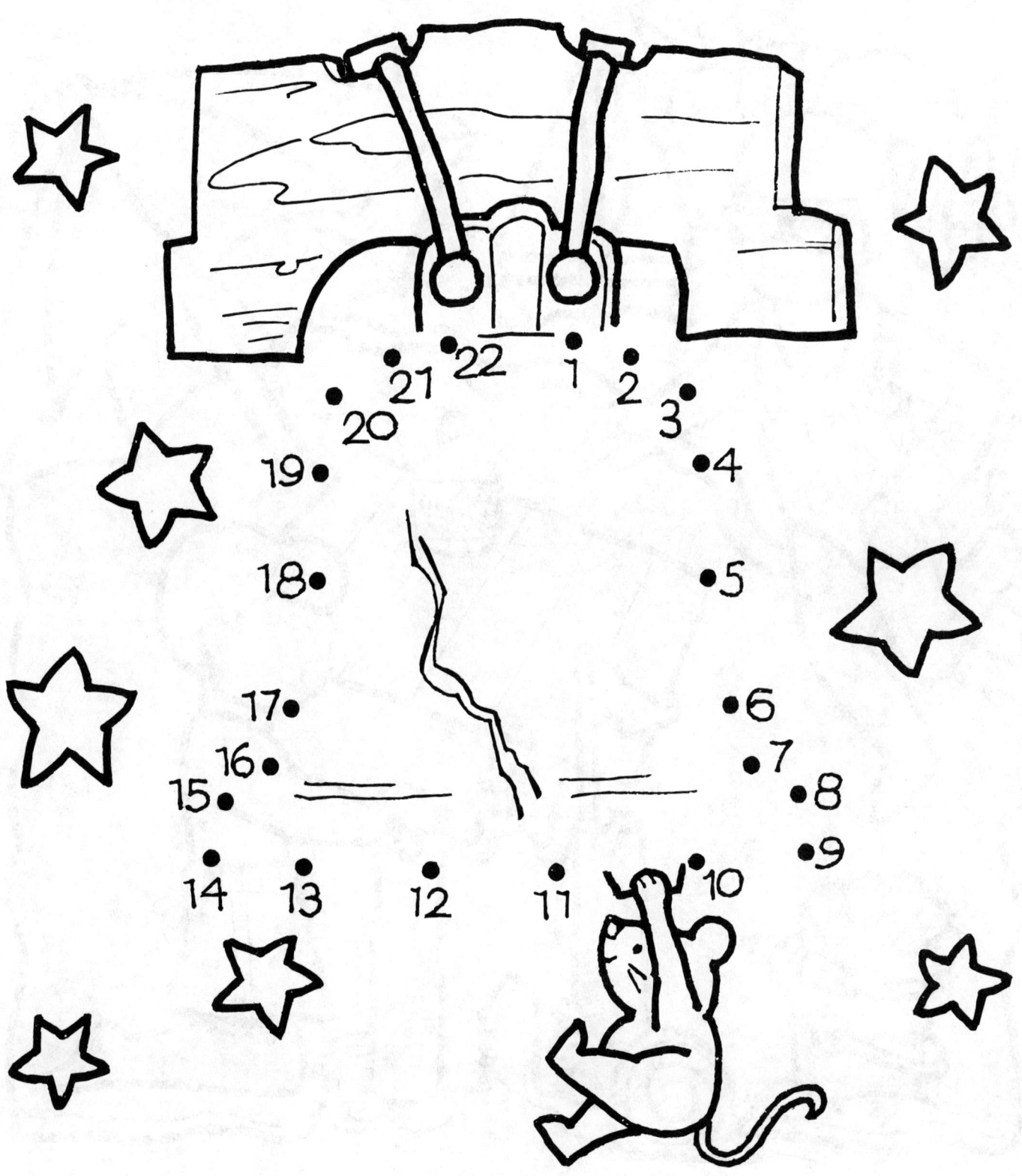

Circle all the things that start with S at the Delaware seashore.

How many Baltimore orioles can you find on the Chesapeake Bay in **Maryland**?

Start at the White House in **Washington, D.C.** and find your way to the Capitol Building.

Match the state shapes with their names.
(Hint—Go back and look at the map of the U.S.A.)

Texas

Florida

Virginia

Tennessee

North Carolina

South Carolina

Georgia

Alabama

Mississippi

Arkansas

Oklahoma

Louisiana

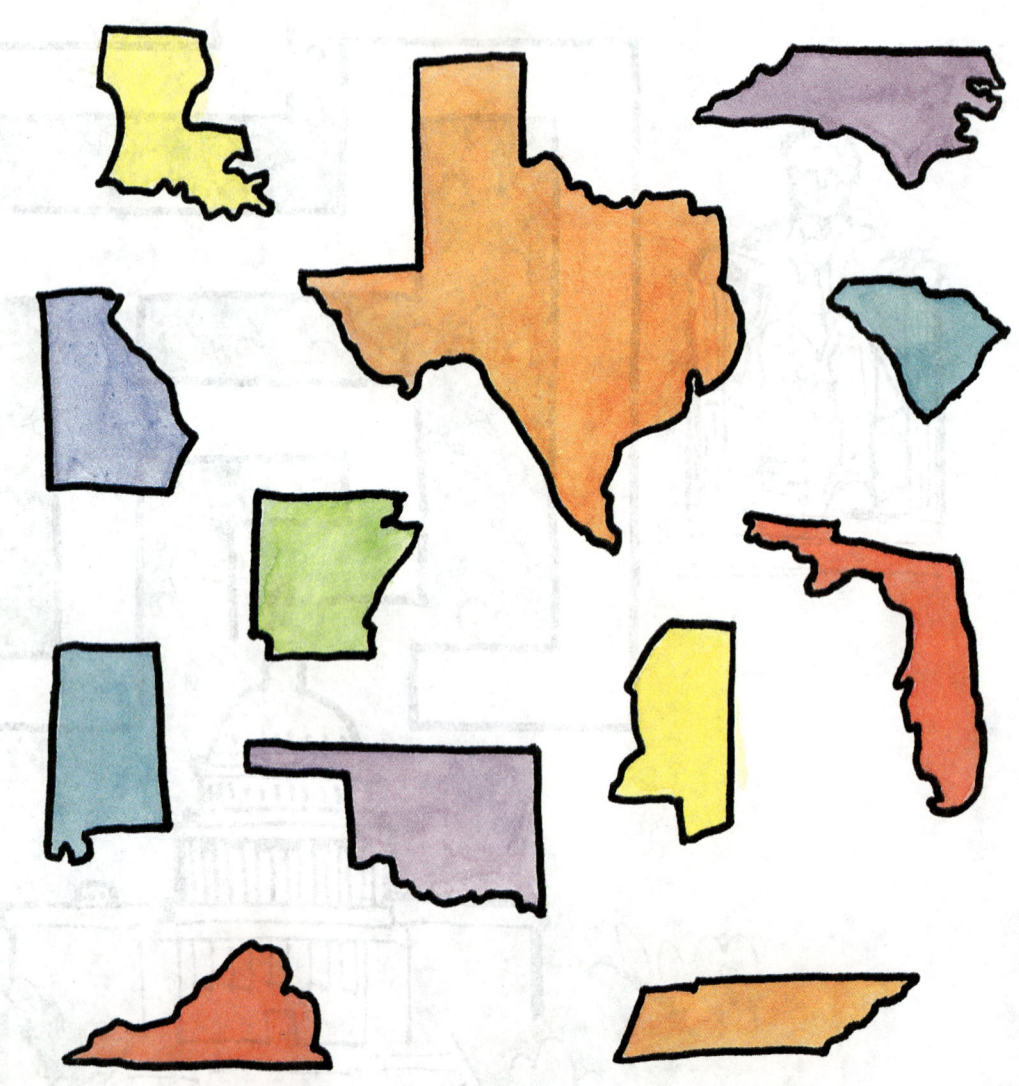

Put an X on the things that should not be blue in the Blue Ridge Mountains of **Virginia**.

What's different between the top and bottom scenes of Charleston, **South Carolina**?

Circle all the things that are round in **Georgia**, the Peach State!

Connect the dots from A to U to see what's blasting off in **Florida**.

Help these animal babies find their mothers in the Great Smoky Mountains of **Tennessee**.

This paddle boat is steaming up the river in Mississippi.

What's wrong with this picture of a New Orleans, **Louisiana**, jazz band?

How many canoe paddles are hidden in this picture of the Buffalo National River in **Arkansas**?

Can you spot six differences between this **Oklahoma** cowboy and his mirror image?

Color in the numbered spaces to see something you might wear in **Texas**.

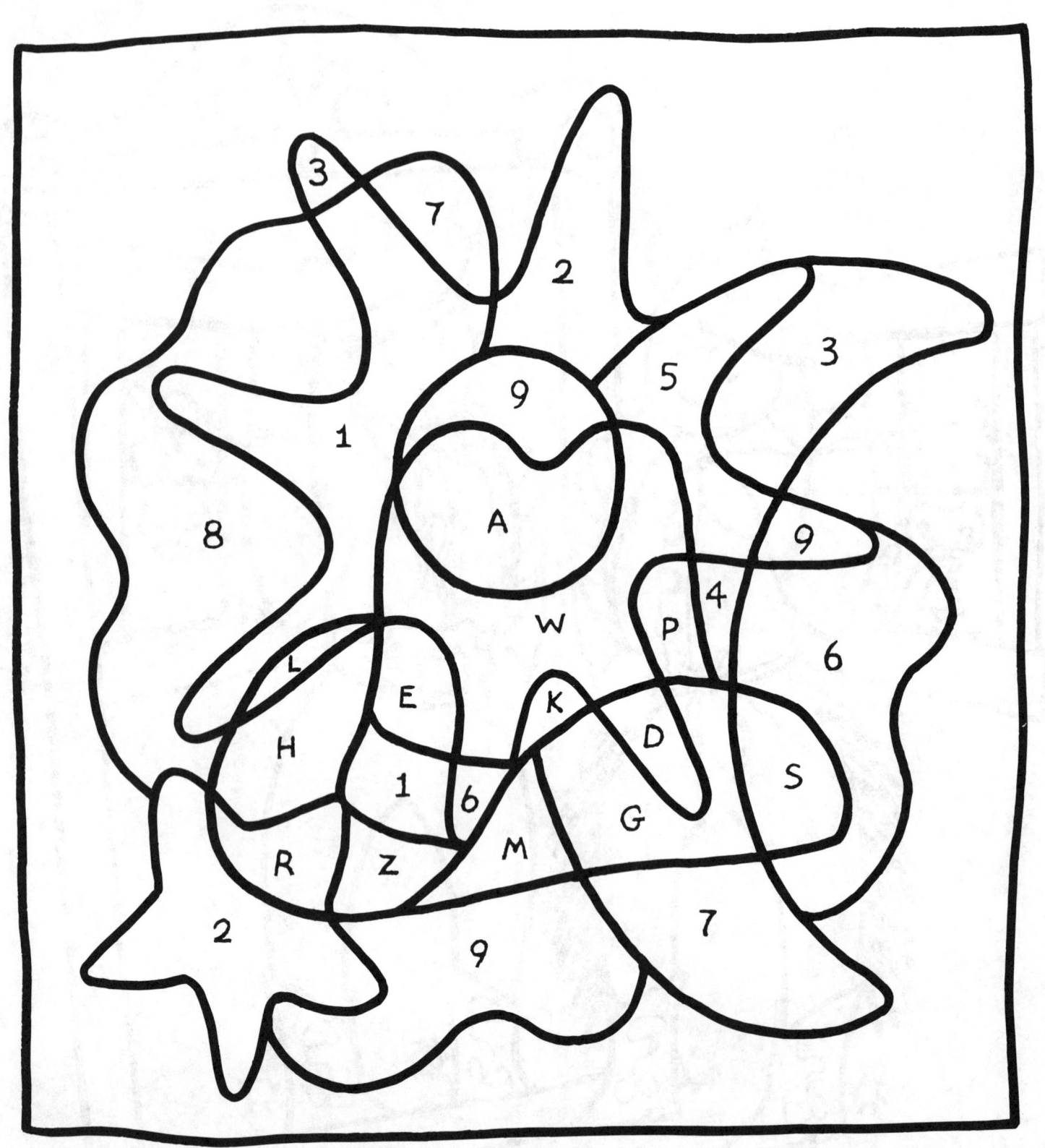

WELCOME
to
The Midwest!

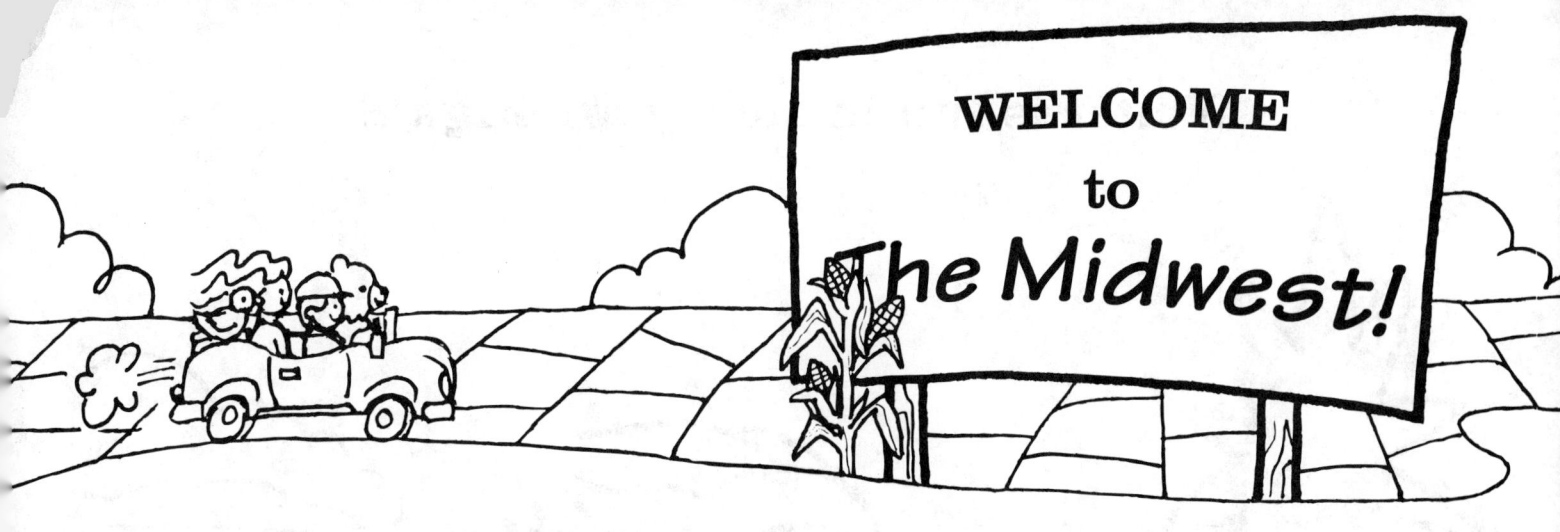

Circle the letters E, I, and O in the names of the midwestern states.

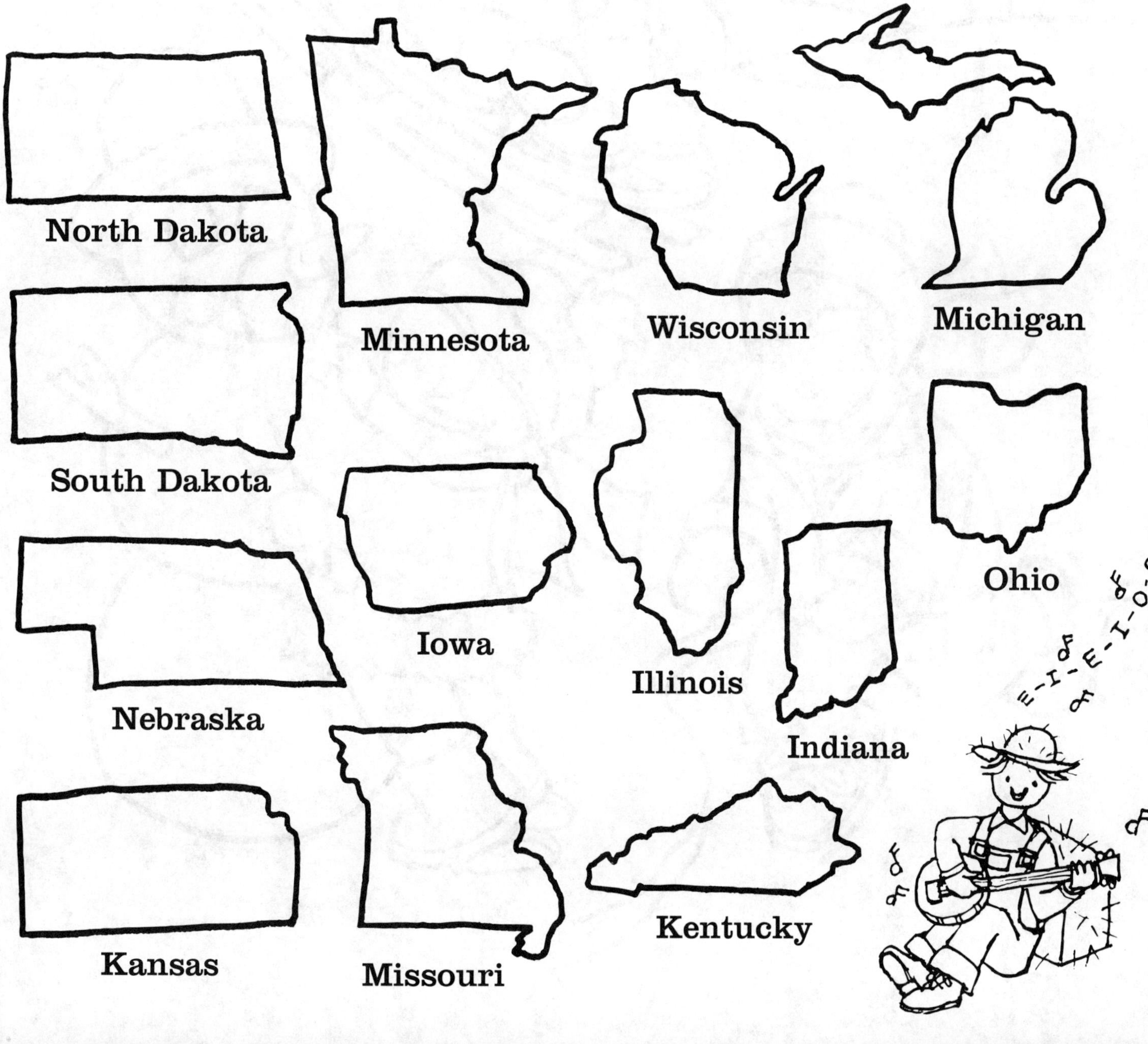
North Dakota
Minnesota
Wisconsin
Michigan
South Dakota
Iowa
Illinois
Ohio
Nebraska
Indiana
Kansas
Missouri
Kentucky
E-I-E-I-O-O-O

Winter is fun in snowy **Michigan!**

Fill in the words. Then use the first letter of each word to find out which sports hall of fame is in Canton, **Ohio**. The first two are done for you.

Something's missing in the Bluegrass fields of **Kentucky**! Fill in the missing parts.

Vroom!
Color in the cars at the races in **Indiana**.

Can you find the letters A to F hidden in the Chicago, **Illinois**, skyline?

What famous landmark rises high above St. Louis, **Missouri**?
Color in the spaces with only one dot to find out.

It's time to rise and shine on this Iowa farm!

Circle the hidden pancakes, syrup, frying pan, egg, and juice so this **Wisconsin** lumberjack can eat breakfast.

Find all the things that start with L in **Minnesota**, the land of 10,000 lakes.

What's different between the top and bottom scenes of the Badlands in **North Dakota**?

Connect the dots from 1 to 22 to find out who's climbing up Mount Rushmore in South Dakota.

Can you find the hidden food in the Great Plains of **Nebraska**?

What's the state flower of Kansas?
Connect the dots from 1 to 26 to find out.

WELCOME to The West!

Circle the place in the west where four states meet. It's called "Four Corners"!

Put an **X** on all the things that are wrong on this **Colorado** ski slope.

There are four pairs of identical things in this picture of the Great Salt Lake in **Utah**. Can you spot them?

Wyoming is home to many animals.
Draw lines to match the moose, elk, bears,
antelopes, mountain lions, and coyotes.

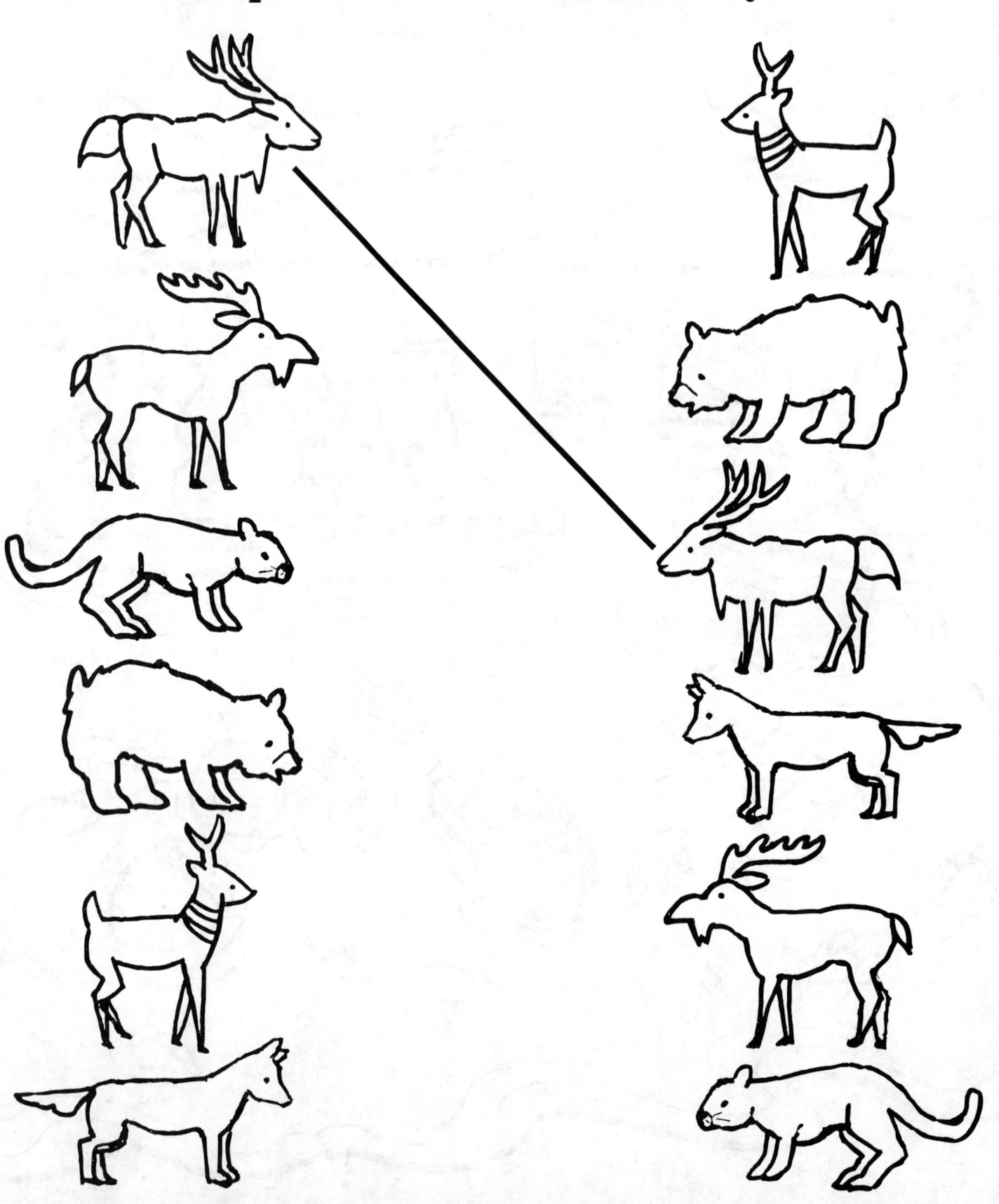

Count the bison
on the Great Plains in **Montana**.

What's the most important crop in **Idaho**?
Fill in the words and use the first letter to find out.
The first two are done for you.

(p) e a r

(o) x

(_) _ _ _ _

(_) _ _ _ _ _

(_) _ _ _

(_) _ _

p   o   _   _   _   _

These **Washington** apple pickers are all mixed up! Can you put the pictures in the right order by numbering them 1 to 4?

Circle all the things that start with B in **Oregon**, the Beaver State.

Can you find the hidden triangles at Hoover Dam in Nevada?

Connect the dots from 1 to 19 to see a famous **California** landmark.

Connect the dots from 1 to 26 to see a prickly plant in Arizona!

Find two cowboys that are the same at this New Mexico rodeo.

It's a dog sled race in **Alaska**!
Help the driver find the way to the finish line.

The surf's up in Hawaii!
Which two pictures are exactly the same?

Every state celebrates the Fourth of July,
our nation's birthday!
Put an X on all the things that are wrong
at this parade.

Can you name the state?
Look at the pictures and read the clues. Then write the state names in the blanks. Use the circled letters to spell out a special message.

You'll find bison on the Great Plains in this state.

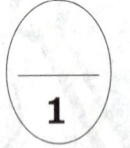

___ ___ (1) ___ ___ ___ ___ ___ ___

This state's state flower is the sunflower.

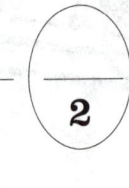

___ ___ (2) ___ ___ ___ ___

The state bird of this state is the goldfinch.

___ (3) ___ ___ ___ (4) ___

The surf's always up in this Pacific Ocean state.

(5) ___ ___ ___ ___ ___

The Baltimore oriole is this state's state bird.

___ ___
 6

Tug boats chug along in the San Francisco Bay in this state.

___ ___
 7

The loon is the state bird for this state with 10,000 lakes.

___ ___
 8

There are a lot of animals in the Great Smoky Mountains in this state.

___ ___
 9

___ ___ ___ ___ ___   ___ ___ ___
 1   5   3   4   3   2   4   3

___ ___ ___ ___ ___   ___ ___ ___ ___ ___ !
 7   8   7   1   6   9   1   2   1   3   9

Where do you live?
Draw a picture of things to see and do in your state.